Graphing the School Cleanup

Suzanne Barchers

CAPSTONE PRESS
a capstone imprint

First hardcover edition published in 2011 by
Capstone Press
151 Good Counsel Drive, P.O. Box 669, Mankato, MN 56002
www.capstonepub.com

Published in cooperation with Teacher Created Materials. Teacher Created Materials is a copyright owner of the content contained in this title.

 This book was manufactured with paper containing at least 10 percent post-consumer waste.

Editorial Credits

Dona Herweck Rice, editor-in-chief; Lee Aucoin, creative director; Sara Johnson, senior editor; Jamey Acosta, associate editor; Neri Garcia and Gene Bentdahl, designers; Stephanie Reid, photo editor; Rachelle Cracchiolo, M.A. Ed., publisher; Eric Manske, production specialist

Library of Congress Cataloging-in-Publication Data
Barchers, Suzanne I.
  Graphing the school cleanup / by Suzanne Barchers.—1st hardcover ed.
    p. cm.—(Real world math)
  Includes index.
  ISBN 978-1-4296-6847-7 (library binding)
 1. Recycling (Waste, etc.)—Graphic methods—Juvenile literature. I. Title. II. Series.
  TD794.5.B3645 2011
  518'.23—dc22   2011001576

Image Credits

Alamy/Jim West, 10; Paul Glendell, 19 (top)
BigStockPhoto/Ernest Prim, 8 (bottom)
Dreamstime/Jojobob, 22 (right); Katrina Brown, 12 (top)
Getty Images/AFL/Doug Pensinger, 23 (top); Leland Bobbe, 11
Shutterstock, 6–7 (bottom); Brandon Blinkenberg, cover (front left), 1 (front left);
    Coprid, cover (front right), 1 (front right); Cynthia Farmer, cover (back), 1
    (back); c.byatt-norman, 20; design56, 12 (bottom left); Dmitriy Shironosov, 6
    (middle); EdBockStock, 7 (front); Frannyanne, 6 (blackboard); Igor Kisselev, 24
    (bottom); Jacek Chabraszewski, 27; Jacob Kearns, 16 (bottles); Jaroslaw
    Grudzinski, 5; Joseph Scott Photography, 26 (bottom); Karin Hildebrand Lau,
    18 (right); Lena Lir, 4 (top); Lukiyanova Natalia/frenta, 24 (top right); Margo
    Harrison, 23 (bottom); Marish, 6 (earth); Mark Payne, 22 (left); Maxstockphoto,
    4 (bottom); Niv Koren, 18 (left); OlgaLis, 13 (right); Panaspics, 26 (top); Pinchuk
    Alexey, 16 (scale); prism68, 14, 19 (bottom); Robert Biedermann, 8 (top); Roman
    Sigaev, 12 (bottom right), 13 (left); Tito Wong, 24 (top left); yalayama, 17
Stephanie Reid, 9

Printed in the United States of America in Stevens Point, Wisconsin.
032011   006111WZF11

Table of Contents

The Big Mess. 4

A Mountain of Cans. 12

A Mountain of Bottles. 16

The Last Steps 22

Problem-Solving Activity. 28

Glossary 30

Index 31

Answer Key 32

The Big Mess

The school year has just begun for the students at Hall School. The students and parents always pick up trash on the playground during the fall. This year it is a big mess!

A late summer storm knocked down a big tree. The storm also blew a lot of trash all over the school.

The teachers help plan the cleanup day. There are a lot of cans and bottles to clean up. They can take them to the city's **recycling center**.

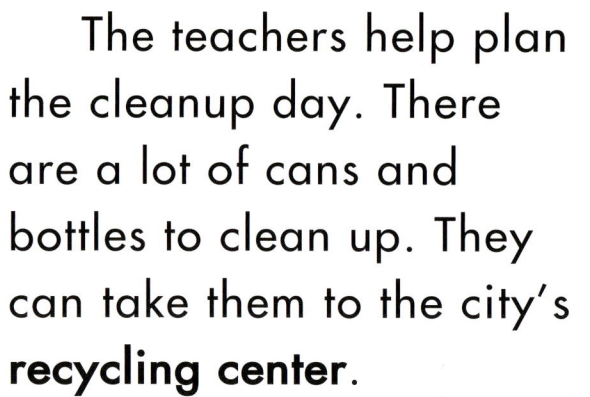

At the recycling center, the cans and bottles can be **exchanged** for money. That will help pay for things at school that need to be fixed.

LET'S EXPLORE MATH

Big City Recycling Center

Container	Payment
aluminum cans	$1.25 per pound
plastic bottles	$1.00 per pound
glass bottles	$0.10 per pound

a. What kind of container pays the least per pound?

b. What kind of container pays the most per pound?

The tree will be chopped up by a machine. The wood chips can be used for some of the play areas.

wood chips

There will be 3 days of work. They will clean up trash on the first day. The parents will cut up the tree on the second day. They will finish on the third day.

Playground Cleanup Schedule

September 7	Clean up the trash
September 14	Cut up the tree
September 21	Paint, finish, and celebrate

On the first day, **volunteers** sign up for teams. The teams start early. One team picks up aluminum cans. Another team picks up plastic. A different team picks up glass.

The teams will take all the collected items to the recycling center. The money the teams earn will be used to buy things that the school needs.

A Mountain of Cans

The volunteers put the empty cans into trash bags. A large trash bag holds about 80 cans. One dad flattens each can with a can crusher.

Then he puts the crushed cans into bags. Each bag now holds more than 300 crushed cans!

LET'S EXPLORE MATH

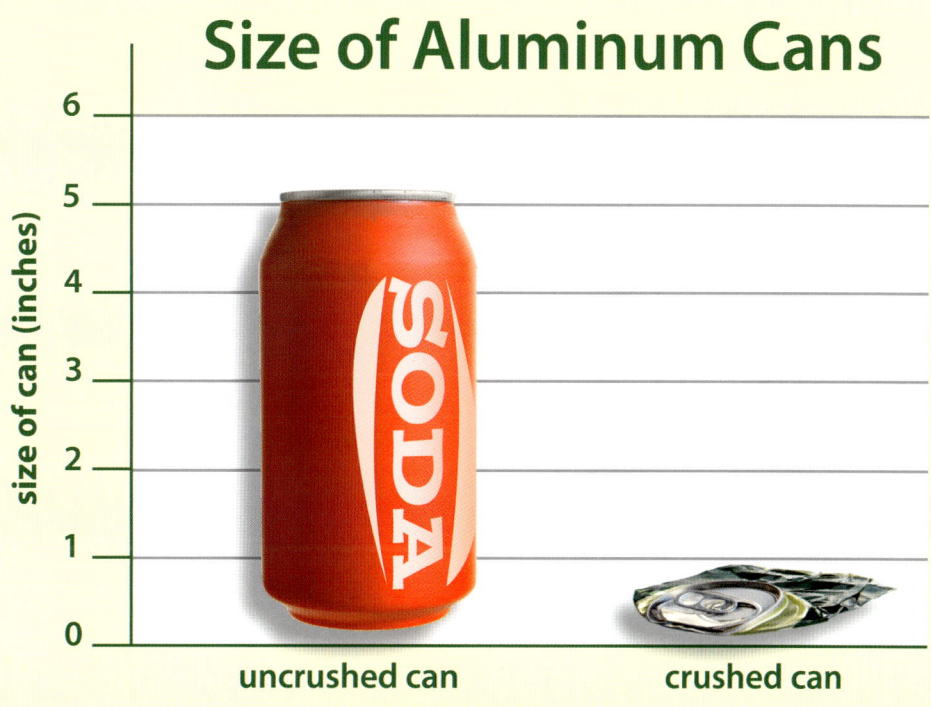

This full-size can is 5 inches tall. About how tall is the crushed can?

The recycling center pays $1.25 for each pound of cans. There are about 32 cans in 1 pound.

The students decide to bring cans from home to recycle too. They bring in 200 pounds of cans. That is a lot of cans!

LET'S EXPLORE MATH

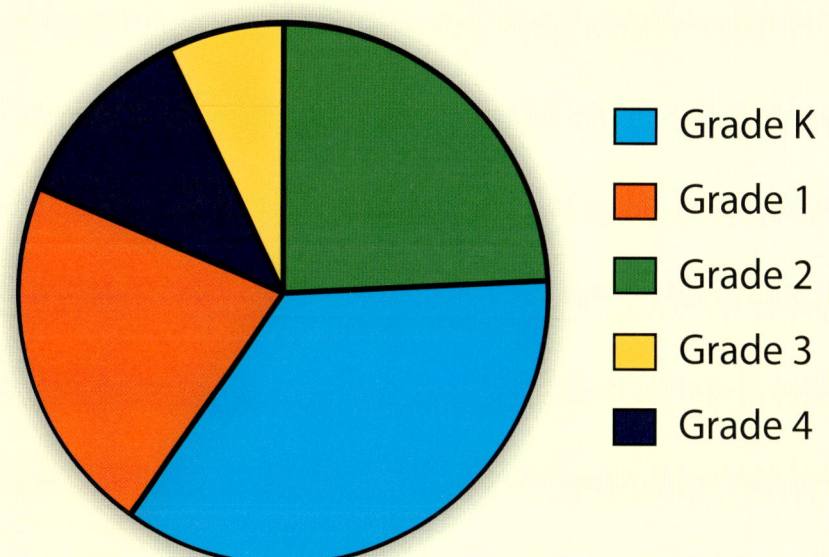

Pounds of Cans by Grade

- Grade K
- Grade 1
- Grade 2
- Grade 3
- Grade 4

a. Which grade brought in the most pounds of cans? How do you know?

b. Which grade brought in the least pounds of cans? How do you know?

A Mountain of Bottles

The students also bring plastic bottles from home. They learn that 8 two-liter plastic bottles weigh about 1 pound.

The students bring in 200 pounds of bottles. That is 1,600 bottles! They take up a lot of space.

The team that picks up glass bottles has a hard job. The adult volunteers help a lot. Some of the bottles are broken. Everyone must wear gloves to protect their hands. They carefully pick up all the small pieces.

The recycling center pays just 10 cents per pound of glass. But glass is heavy. The pounds add up fast.

The students make a **chart** to see how many pounds of each item they collected from home and from the school cleanup. They will use the **data** from the chart to make a graph.

Type of Material	Number of Pounds Collected	Price Paid per Pound
aluminum cans	240	$1.25
plastic bottles	240	$1.00
glass bottles	600	$0.10

The students make a **bar graph** to see how much money they will get from the recycling center. Altogether they will raise $600.00!

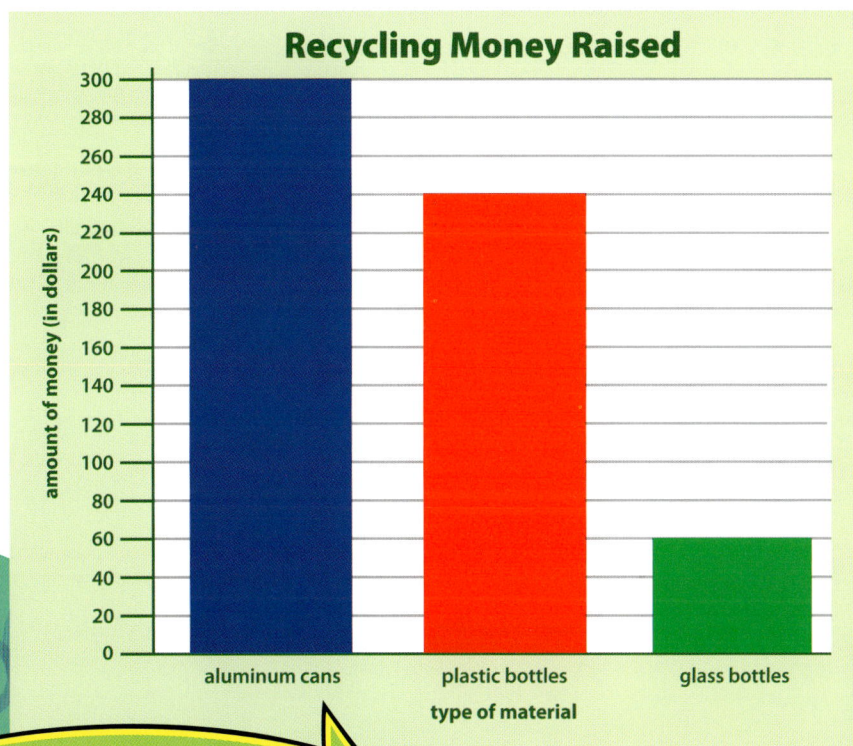

LET'S EXPLORE MATH

Look at the graph above.

a. Which type of material will bring in the most money?

b. How much more money will plastic bottles bring in than glass bottles?

The Last Steps

The teams all come back the next week. The adults cut up the tree. The students pull weeds. A **tree chipper** is used to turn the tree into wood chips.

One group pushes wheelbarrows full of chips to the play areas. Other volunteers rake out the wood chips.

The school has raised a lot of money from their cleanup. Now the students get to vote on what to buy.

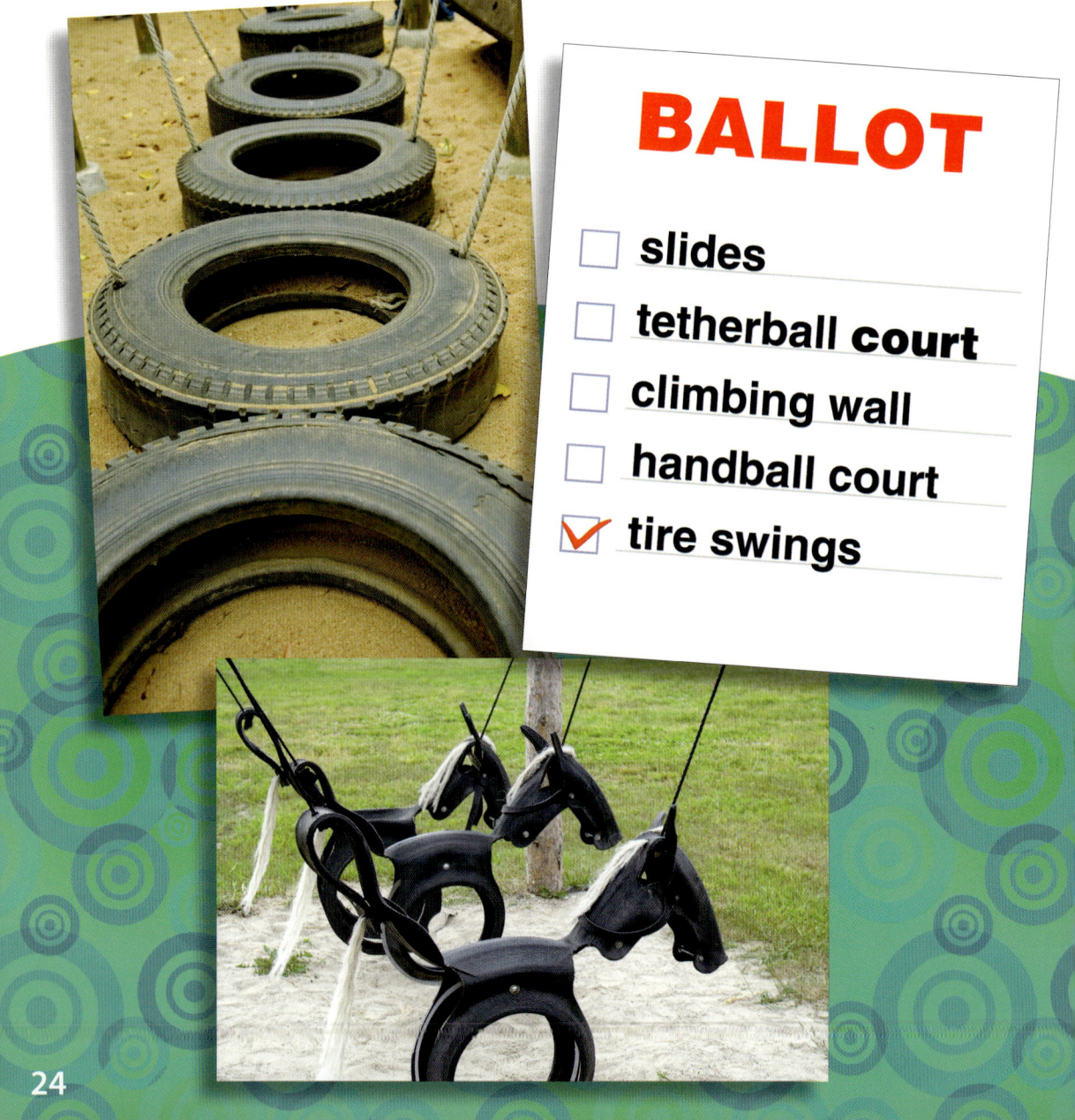

BALLOT

☐ slides
☐ tetherball court
☐ climbing wall
☐ handball court
☑ tire swings

They find out that they can buy great things made from recycled tires. They can even get swings that look like horses!

LET'S EXPLORE MATH

The bar graph shows how the vote turned out.

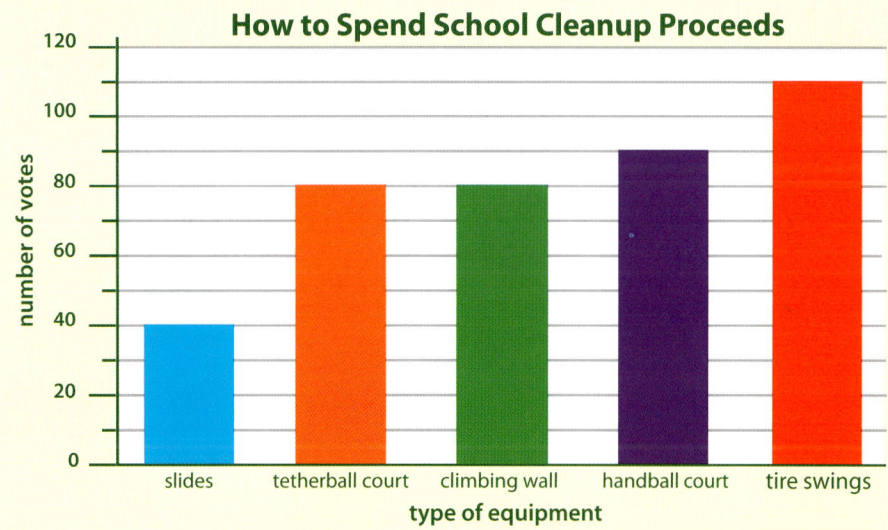

a. How many students wanted slides?

b. There were 2 things that got equal votes. What were they?

c. How many more students wanted a handball court than slides?

The last work day comes. Some parents paint a hopscotch court. Some paint a basketball court. The students help with a new obstacle course. The new tire swings are hung.

Then everyone plays!

A Mountain of Trash

The students at Hollis School want to recycle more. The chart below shows an example of how many pounds of trash a family of 4 throws away each week. The students can use the chart to make a graph to help them plan how to recycle more.

Weekly Trash for Family of Four

Kind of Trash	Pounds Thrown Away
paper	30
food	30
metals	10
glass	10
plastics	10
other	10

Solve It!

a. Use the data in the chart to make a bar graph.

b. Which 2 kinds of waste make the most trash?

c. What types of trash do you want to recycle?

Use the steps below to help you solve the problems.

Step 1: Draw a graph like the one above.

Step 2: Look at the chart. Then add a bar for food.

Step 3: Look at the chart. Then add a bar for metals, glass, plastics, and other.

Step 4: Look at the graph. Find the 2 bars that make the most trash.

Glossary

aluminum—a light metal that is made into cans

bar graph—a graph that uses bars to show information

chart—information that is put in columns and rows so that it is easy to read

court—a space marked for playing a game

data—a collection of information

exchange—to trade one item for another item

recycling center—a place where cans and bottles are processed for reuse

tree chipper—a machine that chops up tree limbs into small pieces

volunteers—people who give their time

Index

aluminum, 7, 10, 13, 20–21

bar graph, 21, 25

chart, 20

court, 24–26

data, 20

pounds, 7, 14–17, 19–20

recycling center, 6–7, 11, 14, 19, 21

tree chipper, 22

volunteer, 10, 12, 18, 23

ANSWER KEY

Let's Explore Math

Page 7:
a. glass bottles

b. aluminum cans

Page 13:
The crushed can is about one inch tall.

Page 15:
a. Grade K; It is the largest space on the graph.

b. Grade 3; It is the smallest space on the graph.

Page 21:
a. aluminum cans

b. $180.00

Page 25:
a. 40 students wanted slides

b. tetherball court and climbing wall

c. 50 more students

Pages 28–29:

Problem-Solving Activity

a.
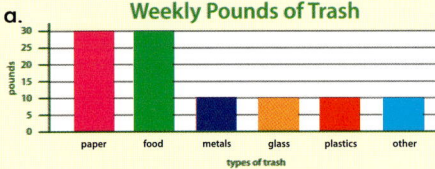

b. paper and food

c. Answers will vary.